To Talitha Ruth

When you were small,

I would tuck you into your crib and say goodnight.

Then as I stepped away, I could hear you mulling over what you'd heard—

"Ma-ma . . . Da-da . . . mo-o-O-OH, D'SUS!"

You've outgrown baby talk now.

But may you never outgrow the truth.

To Caitlin and Emily Roberts

with love, D. A.

Most of All, Jesus Loves You!

Text copyright © 2004 by Noël Piper

Illustrations copyright © 2004 by Debby Anderson

Published by Crossway Books

        a publishing ministry of Good News Publishers

        1300 Crescent Street

        Wheaton, Illinois 60187

Cover design: David LaPlaca

Cover illustration: Debby Anderson

First printing 2004

Printed in USA

Library of Congress Cataloging-in-Publication Data

Piper, Noël, 1947–

   Most of all, Jesus loves you! / Noël Piper ; [illustrated by Debby Anderson].

     p. cm.

   Summary: Every night before bed, a mother reassures her children that they are loved by their family, their friends, and by Jesus.

    ISBN 13: 978-1-58134-630-5 (hc : alk. paper)

    ISBN 10: 1-58134-630-1

   [1. Bedtime—Fiction. 2. Love—Fiction. 3. Christian life—Fiction.] I. Anderson, Debby, ill.II. Title.

PZ7.P6366Mo 2004

[E]—dc22   2004007760

LB		17	16	15	14	13	12	11	10	09	08	07
17	16	15	14	13	12	11	10	9	8	7	6	5	4	3

MOST OF ALL, JESUS LOVES YOU!

NOËL PIPER ILLUSTRATED BY DEBBY ANDERSON

CROSSWAY BOOKS

WHEATON, ILLINOIS

Every night Mama gives me a big hug and a kiss.

Every night she tucks my favorite quilt around me.

Every night she says, "Remember . . .

Mama loves you, and Daddy loves you.

Your brother loves you, and your sister loves you.

Your grandma loves you,
and your grandpa loves you.

Your aunts and uncles love you,
and your cousins love you.

Then every night Mama says,
"Good night, and remember . . .